Dad Jokes

The best collection of hilariously bad Dad jokes

Table of Contents

Introduction

Thank you for taking the time to pick up this book of the very best Dad jokes!

This book contains hundreds of the best, most hilarious, and punny Dad jokes you will ever encounter.

Enjoy sharing these jokes with your friends and family and making them cringe at your new-found humor!

Once again, thanks for choosing this book, I hope you enjoy it!

The best collection of hilariously bad Dad jokes

Did you hear about the restaurant on the moon?

Great food, no atmosphere.

Dad, did you get a haircut?

No, I got them all cut.

What do you call a fake noodle?

An Impasta.

How many apples grow on a tree?

All of them.

What do you get if you put a duck in a cement mixer?

Quacks in the pavement.

Did you know vampires aren't real?

Unless you Count Dracula.

Why did the coffee file a police report?

It got mugged.

Dad, can you put my shoes on?

No, I don't think they'll fit me.

Why did the scarecrow win an award?

Because he was outstanding in his field.

I used to think I was indecisive. Now, I'm not so sure

What's large, grey, and doesn't matter?

An irrelephant.

I've been saying "mucho" quite a lot when talking to my Hispanic friends.

It means a lot to them.

I just got hired at a company that makes bicycle wheels.

I'm the spokesperson.

I'll call you later.

Don't call me later, call me Dad!

Why couldn't the bicycle stand up by itself?

It was two tired.

The shovel was a ground-breaking invention.

Two goldfish are in a tank. One says to the other: "Do you know how to drive this thing?"

What do you call a man with a rubber toe?

Roberto.

What do you call a fat psychic?

A four-chin teller.

The rotation of earth really makes my day.

I thought about going on an all almond diet.

But that's just nuts.

What's brown and sticky?

A stick.

I used to work in a shoe recycling store.

It was sole destroying.

What do you call a bee that can't make up his mind?

A maybe.

"Doc, all my 5 kids want to be valets when they grow up!"

Doctor: "Wow! That's the worst case of parking son's disease I've ever seen."

What kind of vitamin improves your eyesight?

Vitamin see.

I was in a band during the 80s called 'The Prevention'.

We were better than the Cure.

What are terminators called when they retire?

Exterminators.

What do you call a ginger kid who's good at martial arts?

The Carroty Kid.

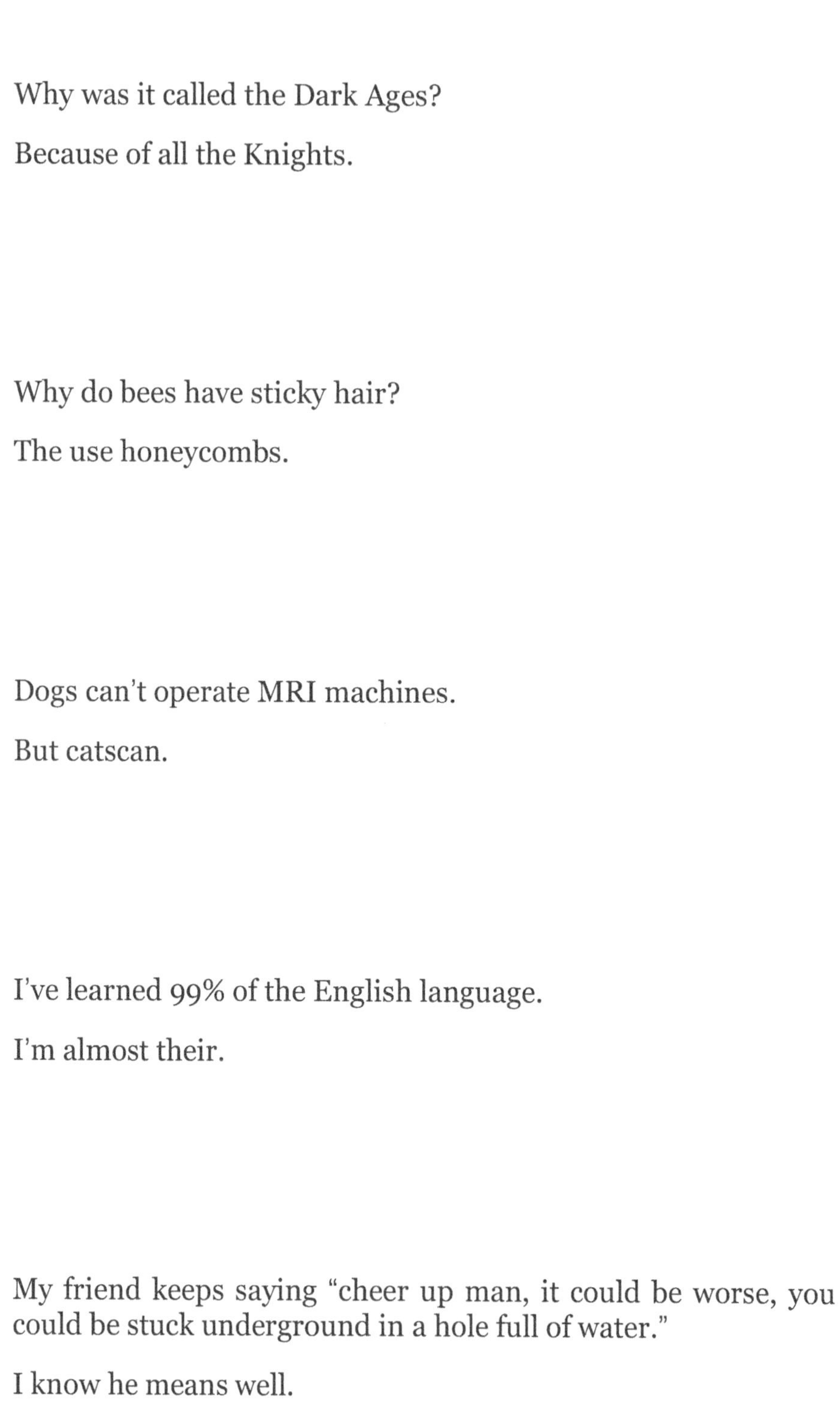

Why was it called the Dark Ages?

Because of all the Knights.

Why do bees have sticky hair?

The use honeycombs.

Dogs can't operate MRI machines.

But catscan.

I've learned 99% of the English language.

I'm almost their.

My friend keeps saying "cheer up man, it could be worse, you could be stuck underground in a hole full of water."

I know he means well.

I love jokes about eyes.

The cornea the better.

I lost 20% of my couch.

Ouch.

My wife didn't believe me when I said that I would give our daughter a silly name.

So, I decided to call her Bluff.

Doctor: Do you want the good news or the bad news?

Patient: Good news, please.

Doctor: We're naming a disease after you…

What type of bagel can fly?

A plain bagel.

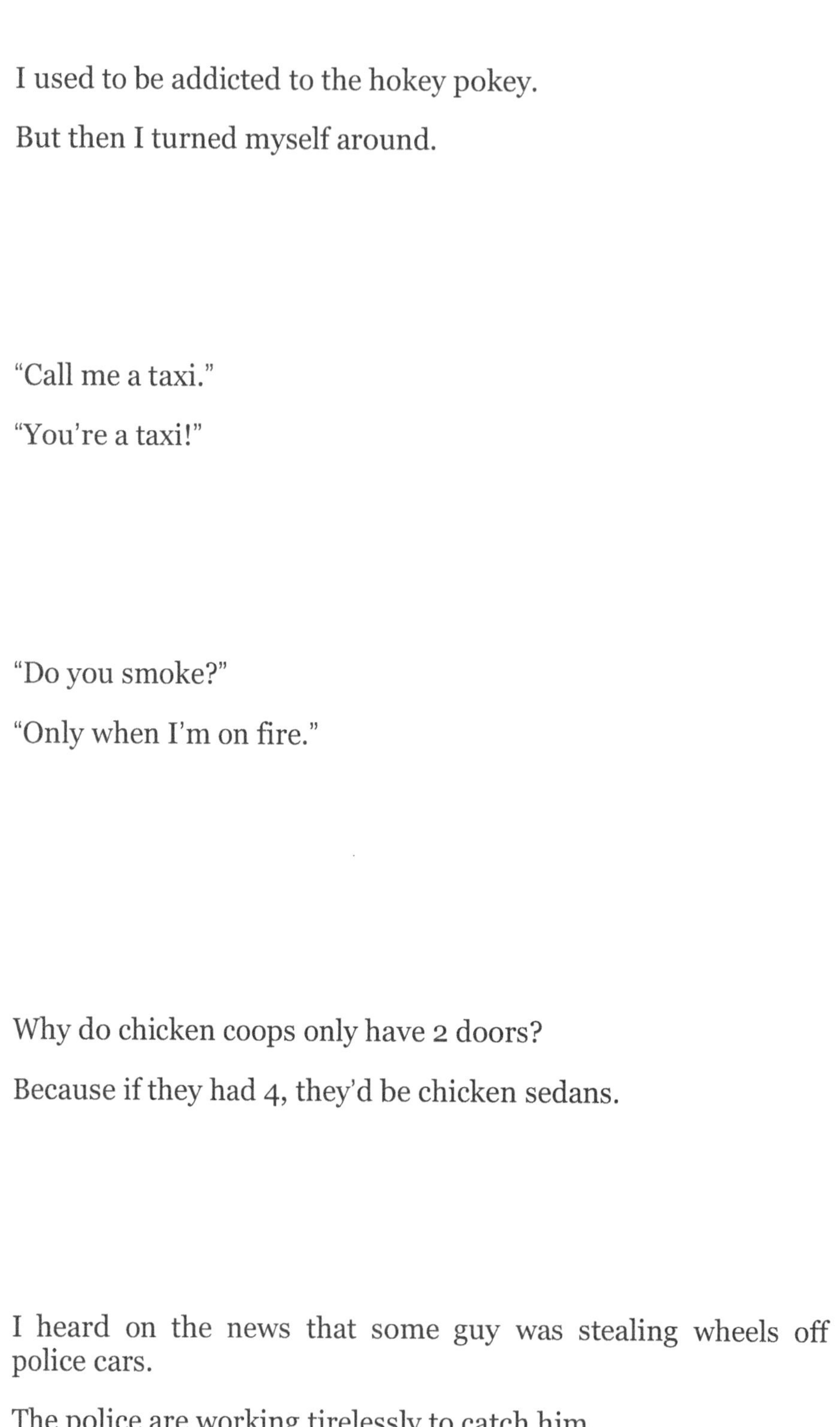

I used to be addicted to the hokey pokey.

But then I turned myself around.

"Call me a taxi."

"You're a taxi!"

"Do you smoke?"

"Only when I'm on fire."

Why do chicken coops only have 2 doors?

Because if they had 4, they'd be chicken sedans.

I heard on the news that some guy was stealing wheels off police cars.

The police are working tirelessly to catch him.

It's a 5-minute walk from my house to the pub.

It's a 35-minute walk from the pub to my house.

The difference is staggering.

I broke my finger last week...

On the other hand, I'm okay.

Why are Irish bankers so successful?

Because their capital is always Dublin.

Why do you pronounce "queue" as "q"?

Because the other letters are waiting in line.

"Dad, can you tell me what a solar eclipse is?"

"No sun."

What do you call a belt made of watches?

A waist of time.

Justice is a dish best served cold.

Because if it was served warm it would be justwater.

In college I was so broke I couldn't afford the electricity bill.

Those were the darkest days of my life.

What do you say to your sister when she's crying?

Are you having a crisis?

You know what the best part of Switzerland is?

Well, the flag is a big plus.

What's orange and sounds like a parrot?

A carrot.

What's brown and rhymes with snoop?

Dr. Dre

I just found out I'm color blind.

The diagnosis came completely out of the purple.

How do you make holy water?

You boil the hell out of it.

Why are mountains funny?

Because they're hill areas.

On our 9th date, my girlfriend and I went to see the new Batman film.

Our dates can be summarized as follows: dinner, dinner, dinner, dinner, dinner, dinner, dinner, dinner, Batman.

Never marry a tennis player…

Love means nothing to them!

As I put my car in reverse, I thought to myself…

"This takes me back."

A pun walks into a bar, ten people die on the spot.

Pun in, ten dead.

Therapist: "Your wife has complained that you never buy her flowers. What do you say to that?"

Man: "To be honest, I had no idea my wife sold flowers."

What does a house wear?

Address.

What do you say to comfort an English teacher?

There, they're, their.

What's the difference between a guy with formal wear on a bicycle, and a guy with casual wear on a unicycle?

Attire.

A guy tried to sell me a mirror, but I knew it was a scam.

I could see right through it.

I used to hate facial hair.

But then it grew on me.

My son's math teacher called him average.

I just think he's mean.

What do you call fake potatoes?

Imitaters.

I have a pen that can write underwater.

It can also write other words too.

We all know Albert Einstein was a genius…

But his brother Frank was a monster.

DO NOT spell the word "part" backwards.

It's a "trap".

Why can't your nose be 12 inches long?

Because then it would be a foot.

People are usually shocked when they find out I'm not a very good electrician.

I hate it when people say age is only a number.

Age is clearly a word.

What weighs less than blue?

Light blue.

Will glass coffins ever become popular?

Remains to be seen.

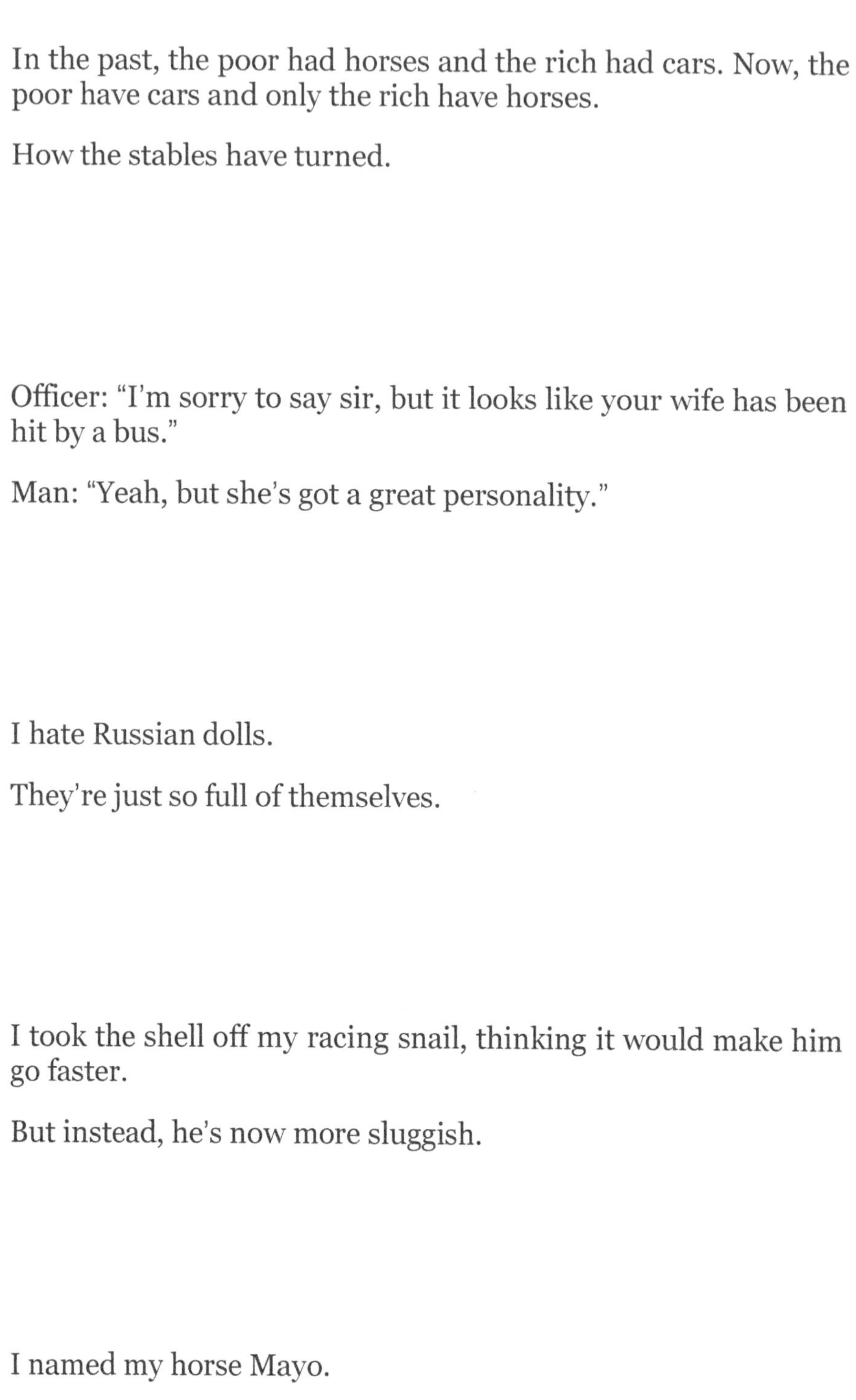

In the past, the poor had horses and the rich had cars. Now, the poor have cars and only the rich have horses.

How the stables have turned.

Officer: "I'm sorry to say sir, but it looks like your wife has been hit by a bus."

Man: "Yeah, but she's got a great personality."

I hate Russian dolls.

They're just so full of themselves.

I took the shell off my racing snail, thinking it would make him go faster.

But instead, he's now more sluggish.

I named my horse Mayo.

Mayo neighs.

When is a car not a car?

When it turns into a driveway.

Some people have trouble sleeping…

But I can do it with my eyes closed.

Why is Cinderella bad at football?

Because she's always running away from the ball.

If you build a man a fire, he will be warm for a day.

If you set a man on fire, he will be warm for the rest of his life.

Guys, to be Frank. I would have to change my name.

How do you get a farm girl to like you?

A tractor.

People think being a waiter isn't a respectable job. But hey, it puts food on the table.

It takes guts to be an organ donor.

Stephen King has a son named Joe.

I'm not joking, but he is.

Why are Saturday and Sunday the strongest days of the week?

The rest are weekdays.

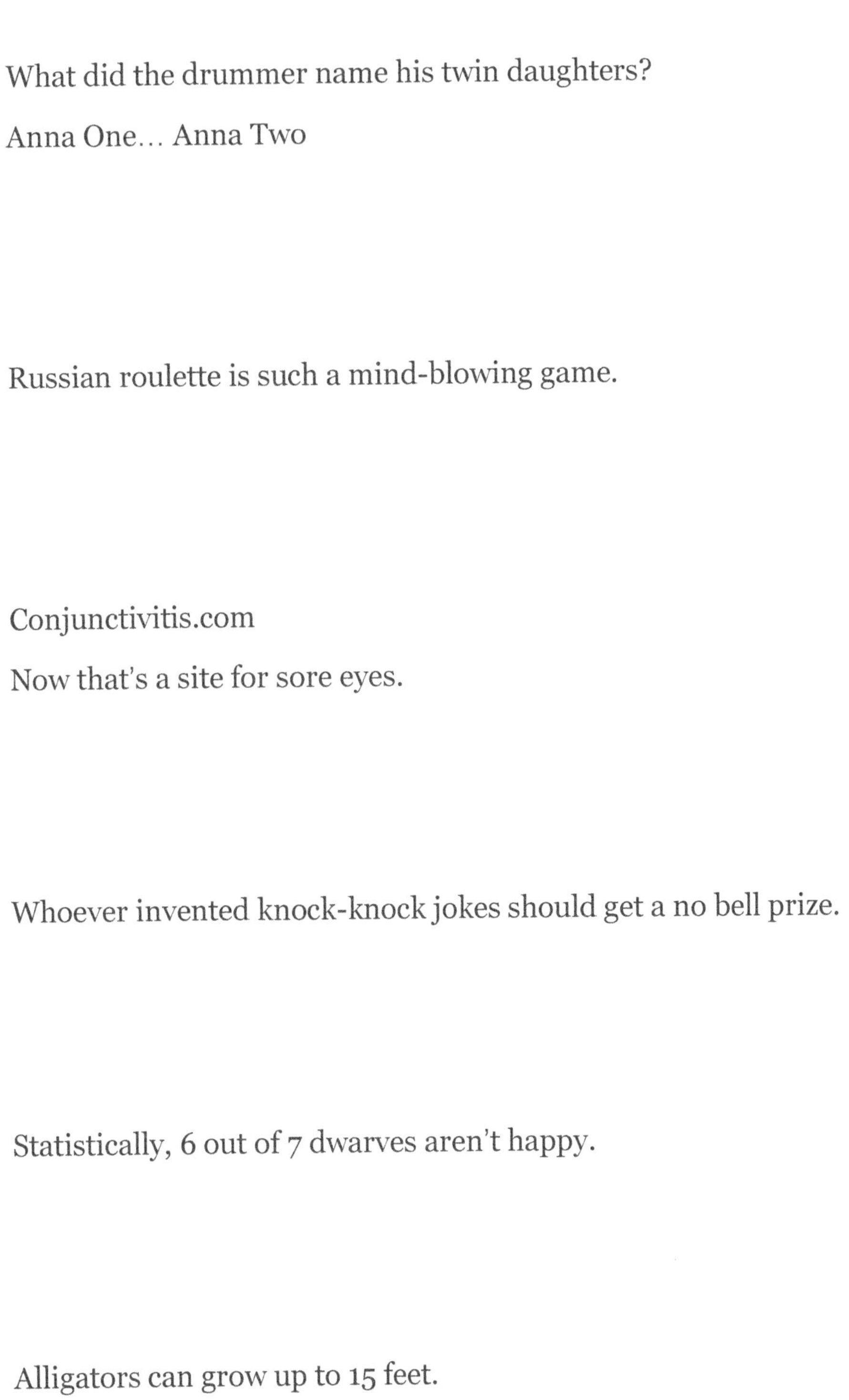

What did the drummer name his twin daughters?

Anna One… Anna Two

Russian roulette is such a mind-blowing game.

Conjunctivitis.com

Now that's a site for sore eyes.

Whoever invented knock-knock jokes should get a no bell prize.

Statistically, 6 out of 7 dwarves aren't happy.

Alligators can grow up to 15 feet.

Most only have 4 though.

What's the difference between a hippo and a zippo?

One is really heavy and the other is a little lighter.

Do you know what's cool?

Winter.

What fish is the best fighter?

The swordfish.

What do you call a bunny without a carrot?

Hungry.

A single glance tells me if somebody is lying.

It's the fact that they're horizontal that gives it away.

Cliffhanger endings are incredibly frustrating. They just

Why aren't cannibals very sociable?

They're all fed up with people.

Why is our nose right in the middle of the face?

Well, it's the scenter.

"Esrowneve" may look like gibberish, but when you put it backwards, it's even worse…

Jokes about communism are only good if everybody gets them.

Son: "Am I adopted?"

Dad: "Not yet, it seems nobody is interested."

When you have a bladder infection… Urine trouble

Geology rocks, but geography is where it's at!

Did you hear about the cheese factory that exploded in France?

There was nothing left but de Brie.

I hate jokes about German sausages.

They're the Wurst.

What did the ocean say to the sailboat?

Nothing, it just waved.

What did the grape do when he got stepped on?

He let out a little wine.

What do you call a zoo that only has one small dog?

A Shih tzu.

I forgot how to throw a boomerang the other day, but then it came back to me.

Cashier: “Would you like the milk in a bag, sir?”

Dad: “No, just leave it in the carton.”

What’s the loudest pet you can get?

A trumpet.

What do you call a deer with no eyes?

No idea.

Why don't crabs share?

Because they're shellfish.

What do you call a hippie's wife?

Mississippi.

I start a new job is Seoul next week. I hope it will be a good Korea move.

What do you call a sketchy Italian neighborhood?

The spaghetto.

Accordion to a recent survey, inserting musical instruments into sentences largely goes unnoticed.

I dig, you dig, we dig, he dig, she dig, they dig.

It's not the best poem, but it's very deep.

It's really hard to say what my wife does for a living.

She sells sea shells by the sea shore.

Why didn't the melons get married?

Because they cantaloupe.

Which is faster, hot or cold?

Hot, because you can catch a cold.

How do you organize a space party?

You planet.

Why are elevator jokes the best?

They work on so many levels.

What do sprinters eat before a race?

Nothing, they fast.

Why do you never see elephants hiding in trees?

Because they're so good at it!

Why did the old man fall in the well?

Because he couldn't see that well.

I like telling Dad jokes. Sometimes he laughs!

The difference between a numerator and a denominator is a short line. Only a fraction of people will understand this.

What's ET short for?

Because he has tiny legs.

I don't play soccer because I enjoy the sport. I'm just doing it for kicks.

What's orange and sounds like a parrot?

A carrot.

What do you call a Donkey that only has 3 legs?

A Wonkey.

Why is Peter Pan always flying?

He Neverlands.

What's a ninja's favorite type of shoes?

Sneakers.

I know a lot of jokes about retired people, but none of them work.

What do Santa's Elves listen to while they work?

Wrap music.

What stinks and rhymes with boo?

You!

Which State is famous for tiny soft drinks?

Minnesota.

What's Forrest Gump's Facebook password?

1forrest1

Why does Snoop Dogg always carry an umbrella?

Fo' Drizzle.

Did you hear about the fire at the campsite?

It was in tents.

Want to hear a joke about paper?

Never mind, it's tear-able.

What's an astronaut's favorite part of a computer?

The space bar.

Where do you learn how to make ice cream?

In sundae school.

Whiteboards are remarkable.

Why did the stadium get so hot after the game?

Because all the fans left.

My friends claim I'm the cheapest person they ever met.

I'm not buying it.

How do you split an ocean in half?

With a sea-saw.

Jail is more than just a word.

It's a sentence.

What do you call a wolf that has things figured out?

Aware wolf.

What do you call a girl in the middle of a tennis court?

Annette.

What do you call a dog with no legs?

You can call him whatever you like, he's never going to come.

My boss hates it when I shorten his name to Dick.

Especially since his name is Steve.

Most puns make me feel numb, but math puns make me feel number.

My wife text messaged me with one word: "Earth."

It meant the world to me.

Why is a panda the most dangerous animal in the world?

Because it eats shoots and leaves.

If I ever find the doctor who screwed up my limb replacement surgery…

I'll kill him with my bear hands.

I left my wife because she was obsessed with counting.

I wonder what she's up to now?

My wife is furious at out next door neighbor who sunbathes nude in her garden.

Personally, I'm on the fence.

They all laughed when I said I wanted to be a comedian.

Well, they're not laughing now.

I was wondering, why does a frisbee appear larger the closer it gets…

Then it hit me.

This morning I tried to catch some fog.

Mist.

I would like to be a millionaire, just like my Dad.

He always wanted to be a millionaire, too.

I can't take my dog to the pond anymore because the ducks keep attacking him.

I guess that's what I get for having a pure bread dog.

Some mornings, I wake up grumpy.

On others, I let her sleep in.

So far, Humpty Dumpty is having a terrible winter.

Which sucks, because he had a great fall.

What did the octopus say to his girlfriend when he proposed?

"Can I have your hand hand hand hand hand hand hand hand in marriage?"

I have a Russian friend who's a sound technician.

And a Czech one too. A Czech one too.

Mahatma Gandhi walked barefoot most of the time, which produced an impressive set of callouses on his feet. He also ate little, which made him frail, and with his odd diet he suffered from bad breath.

This made him a super calloused fragile mystic hexed by halitosis.

What's blue and smells like red paint?

Blue paint.

I'm really upset! Someone stole my limbo stick!

How low can you go?

I've never seen the inside of my ears…

But I've heard good things.

I got mugged by six dwarves last night.

Not happy.

I want to thank everyone for sticking by me while I figured out the meaning of "many."

It means a lot.

I took my dog to the lake today and noticed he floats very well.

He's a very good buoy.

To the guy who invented zero…

Thanks for nothing.

Poop jokes aren't my favorite, but they're a solid number 2.

Thank you student loans for getting me through college.

I don't know how I'll ever repay you!

My girlfriend told me to take the spider out instead of killing it.

We went and had some drinks. Cool guy. Wants to be a web developer.

To whoever stole my antidepressants, I hope you're happy!

I'm fine letting other people dot my i's, but crossing my t's?

That's where I draw the line!

What do you call an underwater dog?

A subwoofer.

Is it just me or are circles pointless?

The average height of a dwarf is 3 feet.

That's a little gnome fact.

Last night, I gave my girlfriend a medieval battle uniform to polish while I went to the pub.

She always said she wanted a night in, shining armor.

I didn't think a chiropractor would improve my posture.

But I stand corrected.

Two goldfish are in a tank. One says to the other: "Do you know how to drive this thing?"

Women call me ugly until they find out how much money I make.

Then they call me ugly and poor.

Why is 6 afraid of 7?

Because 7 is a registered 6 offender.

I told my girlfriend she was drawing her eyebrows too high.

She looked surprised.

The swordfish has few predators in the wild.

Except for the rare penfish, which is said to be mightier.

I just bought my wife an artificial leg for Christmas.

It's not her main present, just a stocking filler.

What do you call a snowman with a six pack?

An abdominal snowman.

My wife and I always laugh about how competitive we are.

But I laugh more.

Studies show that cows produce more milk when they farmer talks to them.

It's a case of in one ear and out the udder.

I went to the zoo and saw a baguette in a cage.

The zookeeper told me it was bread in captivity.

My wife and I were arguing about which vowel is the most important.

I won.

I once swallowed a dictionary.

It gave me thesaurus throat I've ever had.

What word becomes shorter when you add two letters to it?

Short.

It wasn't much fun having a broken neck…

But now I can look back and laugh.

A slice of apple pie is $2.50 in Jamaica and $3.00 in the Bahamas.

These are the pie rates of the Caribbean.

Conclusion

Thanks again for choosing this book!

I hope you've enjoyed this collection of Dad jokes and have had fun sharing them with your friends and family!

If you enjoyed this book, please take the time to leave me a review on Amazon. I appreciate your honest feedback, and it really helps me to continue producing high quality books.

www.ingramcontent.com/pod-product-compliance
Lightning Source LLC
Chambersburg PA
CBHW051734050726
47598CB00003B/1191

* 9 7 8 1 7 6 1 0 3 0 1 2 3 *